Contents

Welcome to Kenya

The Republic of Kenya straddles the equator on the coast of east central Africa. It stretches from the Indian Ocean to the shores of Lake Victoria.

Kenya shares borders with five other African countries: Uganda, Sudan, Ethiopia, Somalia and Tanzania. Part of the short border with Sudan is disputed. Kenya is a modern, independent country with a lively culture.

A varied land

Kenya's landscape is amazingly varied. In a country about twice the size of the US state of Nevada, there are dusty plains, cool highlands, hot springs, mountains, dense forests, tea and coffee plantations, swamps, lakes, rivers, sandy beaches and even glaciers and coral reefs. Kenya is world-famous for its national parks and wildlife reserves. Tourists flock to them from all over the world to enjoy their spectacular scenery and wildlife.

High-rise offices and government buildings fill the centre of Nairobi, the capital city. ▼

The Land

Kenya is a land of geographical contrasts. The eastern side of the country slopes down to the Indian Ocean, while the western side features dramatic highlands, mountains and a breathtaking valley.

The south and west are covered by fertile grasslands and forests. The Great Rift Valley, a vast 30 million-year-old depression, runs through the western side of the country. It is the result of Africa and Arabia moving apart, causing the land between them to drop. The Aberdare mountain range rises up on the eastern rim of the rift. It slopes away towards the east, meeting Kenya's highest mountain, Mount Kenya (5,199 metres). Further east lies the coastal strip that skirts the Indian Ocean. Here are beautiful sandy beaches. Coral reefs lie just offshore.

 Animals and Plants

Kenya's varied landscape is home to animals ranging from the world's biggest land mammals to beautiful tropical birds. Plant life includes rainforest flowers and alpines.

Mammals:
Lion, leopard, cheetah, buffalo, hyena, giraffe, hippopotamus, elephant, rhinoceros, zebra, impala, water buck, bush buck, eland, wildebeest, kudu, warthog, baboon, colobus monkey, fruit bat.

Birds:
Flamingo, cormorant, heron, ibis, egret, fish eagle, kestrel, pelican, vulture, ostrich, secretary bird, bee-eater, flycatcher, sparrowhawk, crane, kingfisher.

Reptiles and amphibians:
Nile crocodile, green mamba, skink, monitor lizard, chameleon.

Plants:
Acacia tree, cedar tree, baobab tree, podo wood, bamboo, tree groundsel, giant lobelia.

◄◄ Giraffes roam across the savannah, or grassland, that covers much of the southern half of Kenya.

Lakes and rivers

Part of Lake Victoria lies within Kenya. The lake is Africa's largest and, after Lake Superior in the USA, the world's second-largest freshwater lake. Lake Turkana (also known as Lake Rudolf), a tenth the size, lies in the north of the country. Many of Kenya's rivers are seasonal, disappearing altogether in dry periods. The longest, the Tana, flows some 700 kilometres from the Aberdare Range and Mount Kenya to the Indian Ocean.

Climate

Kenya's equatorial location means that the daytime temperature changes very little throughout the year. The average daytime temperature in Mombasa, at sea level, is 27–31°C. Nairobi, at an altitude of 1,661 metres, is cooler, with an average daytime temperature of 21–26°C. There are two wet seasons during the year. The 'long rains' last from April to June, when monthly rainfall can exceed 300 millimetres in places. After a warm, dry period, the 'short rains' follow in November and December. January to March is hot and dry.

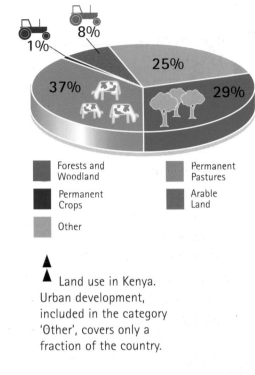

- Forests and Woodland
- Permanent Crops
- Other
- Permanent Pastures
- Arable Land

▲ Land use in Kenya. Urban development, included in the category 'Other', covers only a fraction of the country.

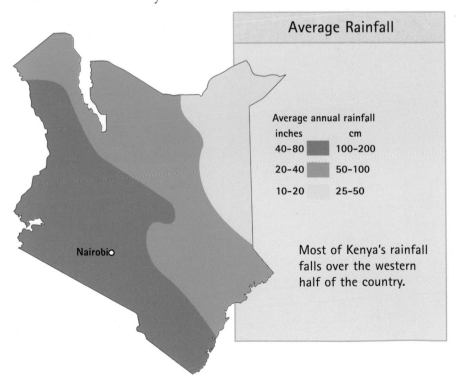

Average Rainfall

Average annual rainfall

inches	cm
40–80	100–200
20–40	50–100
10–20	25–50

Most of Kenya's rainfall falls over the western half of the country.

Nairobi○

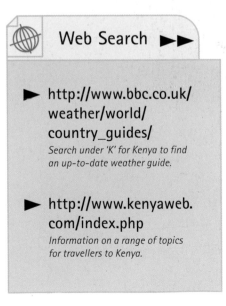

Web Search ►►

► http://www.bbc.co.uk/ weather/world/ country_guides/
Search under 'K' for Kenya to find an up-to-date weather guide.

► http://www.kenyaweb. com/index.php
Information on a range of topics for travellers to Kenya.

The People

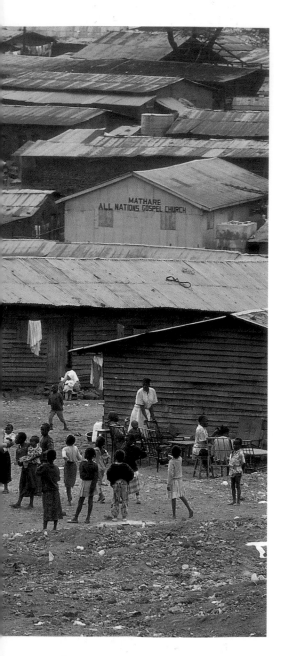

Kenya's population of about 34 million people is composed of 40 different ethnic groups. The most recognizable are the Masai. These tall, slim people wear red wraps and brightly coloured beaded jewellery. The men often carry spears and shields.

Although the Masai belong to Kenya's most famous tribe, they account for less than 2 per cent of the population. The most numerous are the Kikuyu, who number about 6.8 million. Along with the Embu, Mbere, Tharaka and Kamba, they live mainly in the Central Rift highlands.

The Luhya, the second largest group, occupy the area around Lake Victoria. The Masai live a nomadic life mainly along the Tanzanian border. Another nomadic tribe, the Turkana, live mainly in the north-west. The Somali and Oromo tribes are based in the north and north-east. About 98 per cent of Kenya's population are African. The rest are mainly Arab, Indian, Pakistani and British.

▲ Children play outside shanty, or makeshift housing, in a suburb of Nairobi.

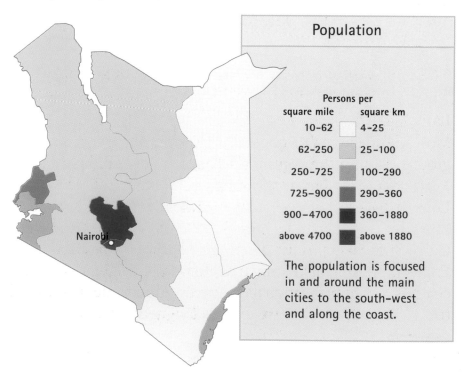

Population

Persons per	
square mile	square km
10–62	4–25
62–250	25–100
250–725	100–290
725–900	290–360
900–4700	360–1880
above 4700	above 1880

Nairobi

The population is focused in and around the main cities to the south-west and along the coast.

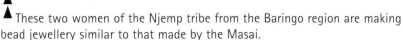
These two women of the Njemp tribe from the Baringo region are making bead jewellery similar to that made by the Masai.

Language

Most of the languages spoken by Kenya's many ethnic groups fall into three groups – Bantu, Nilotic and Cushitic. Most people are Bantu-speaking, including the Kikuyu and Luhya tribes. Nilotic speakers include the Luo, Masai and Kalenjin tribes. The northern Somali and Oromo tribes are Cushitic speakers. Most people also speak Swahili and English. Swahili, also known as Kiswahili, originated on the coast as a common language between Arab traders and local tribes. English was Kenya's official language until it was replaced by Swahili in 1974.

 Ancient History

Some of the earliest humans on Earth lived in East Africa. In 1984, the skeleton of a boy who lived 1.6 million years ago was found on the shore of Lake Turkana. In 2001, the skull of a human-like species called *Kenyanthropus platyops* (meaning flat-faced man of Kenya) about 3.5 million years old was found in the same area.

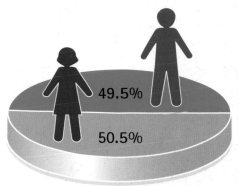

49.5%

50.5%

Female Population 17,083,942

Male Population 16,745,647

There are slightly more women than men in Kenya's population.

 **Web Search** ►►

► http://www.cia.gov/ cia/publications/fact book/geos/ke.html
The Kenya entry in the CIA World Factbook.

Urban and Rural Life

Kenya's population is largely rural. Only about one-third of the people live in towns and cities. From about 1960, the urban population, although small, grew so quickly that the economy was unable to provide enough housing. As a result slum areas have sprung up around the cities, and more than half of Kenya's urban population now lives in poverty.

Most of Kenya's towns and cities grew from settlements founded thousands of years ago. The capital, Nairobi, is an exception. Nairobi is just over 100 years old. It was created in May 1899 where engineers building the Mombasa to Kampala railway between Kenya and Uganda stopped to plan the route ahead. As a young city, Nairobi lacks the historic buildings of many other Kenyan towns and cities.

 Health

Life expectancy and infant survival rates in Kenya have been improved since the 1960s by better health care. However, measles still kills thousands of Kenyans every year. A campaign begun in 2002 has vaccinated 97.9% of Kenyan children against measles. Kenya also suffers outbreaks of malaria, the main killer disease all over sub-Saharan Africa.

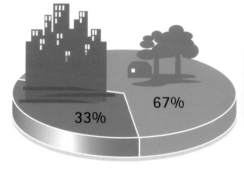

Percentage of Population Living in Urban Areas

Percentage of Population Living in Rural Areas

▲ About two-thirds of Kenya's people live in rural areas, living off the land.

◄◄ Mombasa, on the coast, grew as a trading town. Many of the streets around its harbour are narrow and filled with vehicles and traders' stalls.

In rural areas, water is hard to find. Here, villagers are filling plastic barrels with water from the bed of a dried-up river.

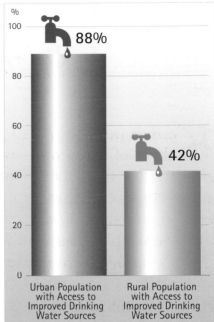

 88%

 42%

Urban Population with Access to Improved Drinking Water Sources	Rural Population with Access to Improved Drinking Water Sources

▲ Less than 1 in 3 people in rural areas have access to fresh drinking water. In many rural areas, water must be boiled to kill germs before it is safe for drinking.

Rural women

Women in rural areas have a particularly difficult time. Nearly half of the farms in western Kenya are managed by women on their own. They have no access to the labour-saving devices that many urban people take for granted. From housework to working the land, everything is done by hand. A typical day on a rural farm begins as early as 5.00 a.m. and does not end until perhaps 10.00 p.m.

🌐 Web Search ▶▶

▶ http://www.fao.org/ giews/english/basedocs/ ken/kenpop1e.stm
A population density map for Kenya from the United Nations Food and Agriculture Organization.

▶ http://unstats.un.org/ unsd/demographic/social/
Select 'water supply and sanitation' for the percentages of urban and rural people with access to clean drinking water, from the United Nations Statistics Division.

Farming and Fishing

The majority of the Kenyan population is involved in agriculture. Most are subsistence farmers, growing just enough for themselves and their families. In places where it is too dry to grow crops, animals are kept. Agriculture on an industrial scale is very important for the economy. The tea industry is the country's biggest export earner.

Highland and lowland crops

Different crops are grown in the highland and lowland regions of the country. Coffee, tea, wheat and pyrethrum are grown in the highlands. Kenya is one of the world's largest suppliers of pyrethrum, a natural pesticide. Coconuts, pineapples, cashew nuts, cotton and sugar cane are grown on lower ground. Sisal and corn are grown in both regions. Livestock farming produces beef, pork, poultry and eggs.

Agricultural exports

Coffee, tea and horticultural products such as cut flowers, fruit and vegetables account for more than half of Kenya's exports. Only India and China produce more tea than Kenya. However, a country that depends so heavily on agriculture can suffer economically if crops fail or yields decline because of bad weather, climate change, pests or diseases. The whole agricultural industry in Kenya declined during the 1990s because of long periods of drought. At the same time, Kenya's growing population places increasing demands on agriculture to supply its needs. The demand for bread has grown so quickly that the amount of wheat required outstripped supplies in the mid-1990s, leading to shortages and the need to import.

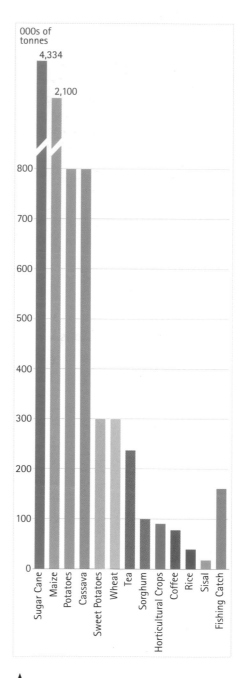

▲ Kenya's annual farming and fishing production by weight.

Fishing

Kenya's fishing industry is dominated by freshwater fish caught in its lakes. Nile perch are caught in Lake Turkana. Lake Naivasha produces black bass and tilapia. Lake Victoria yields tilapia, cichlids and Nile perch. The Nile perch were introduced to Lake Victoria to control mosquitoes, which deposit their eggs in fresh water.

▲ A stall in the fruit and vegetable market in Nairobi. Local farmers bring their products to the market as soon as they are harvested.

Farming and Crops

Only about 15 per cent of Kenya's land is fertile enough to be farmed.

Nairobi

Cattle
Coffee
Tea
Sisal

Crop Zones

Maize
Rice
Wheat
Millet
Sorghum
Barley
Sugar Cane
Cassava
Potatoes

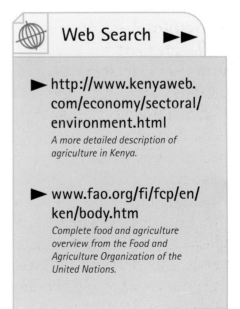

Web Search ►►

► http://www.kenyaweb.com/economy/sectoral/environment.html
A more detailed description of agriculture in Kenya.

► www.fao.org/fi/fcp/en/ken/body.htm
Complete food and agriculture overview from the Food and Agriculture Organization of the United Nations.

13

Resources and Industry

Kenya's most important natural resources are its land and wildlife. The tourist industry is a major foreign-income earner. There are few mineral resources. Mining accounts for less than 1 per cent of Kenya's Gross Domestic Product (GDP).

The main minerals mined or quarried are soda ash, fluorspar and kaolin. Limestone deposits along the coast are also mined for the cement-making industry. A small amount of gold and greenstone gems are produced. Soda ash quarried at Lake Magadi is used for glassmaking. Fluorspar is mined mainly for export, for use in steel-making and in the production of fluorine gas. Kaolin is a soft white clay used in a variety of different industries. Although Kenya has no major oil fields of its own, its refineries process oil from other countries.

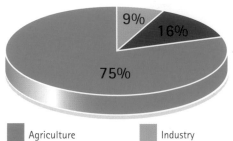

9%
16%
75%

Agriculture   Industry

Services

▲ The majority of Kenya's labour-force works in agriculture.

Manufacturing Industry

Manufacturing contributes about 14 per cent of GDP. It mainly involves processing agricultural products to make tea, coffee, sugar, paper and leather goods. Some household goods, vehicle parts and farm tools are manufactured locally on a small scale, too.

◄◄ Most small factories and workshops burn wood in furnaces to provide fuel rather than use expensive oil or coal as an energy source.

Energy

Economic development depends on energy. Most of Kenya's energy is generated by hydro-electric power plants and most of it is consumed in the two largest cities, Nairobi and Mombasa. However, prolonged droughts reduce the amount of water available for power generation. Electricity was rationed for the two years up to 2001 because of droughts. Oil-fired power stations need far less water than hydro-electric power stations, but the oil to fuel them has to be imported at great expense. Geothermal, wind and solar power, which do not need expensive imported fuel, are being studied and developed.

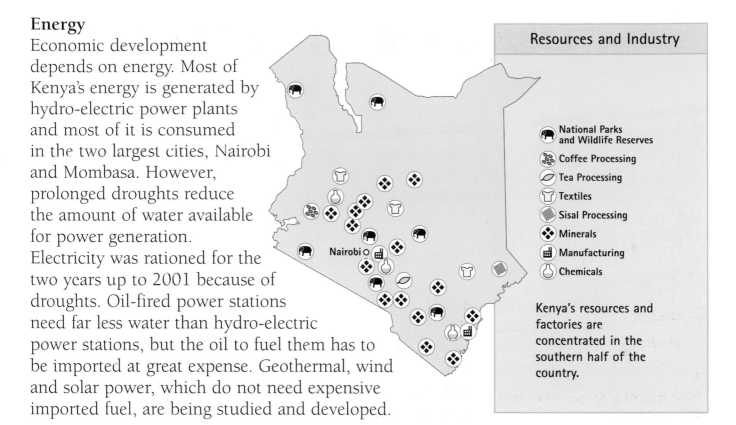

Resources and Industry

- National Parks and Wildlife Reserves
- Coffee Processing
- Tea Processing
- Textiles
- Sisal Processing
- Minerals
- Manufacturing
- Chemicals

Kenya's resources and factories are concentrated in the southern half of the country.

Nairobi

◄◄ A geothermal energy plant in the Rift Valley. Holes are bored in the ground to reach hot rocks deep below the surface. Cold water is piped down and the hot water or steam pumped to the surface, where it is used to make electricity.

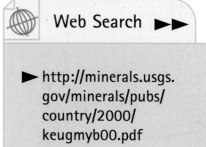

Web Search ►►

► http://minerals.usgs. gov/minerals/pubs/ country/2000/ keugmyb00.pdf
Kenya's mineral production figures from the US Geological Survey.

Transport

Kenya's extensive road and railway networks are important not only to Kenya itself, but also to its landlocked neighbours. Uganda, Burundi, Rwanda and the Democratic Republic of Congo (formerly Zaire) use Kenya to reach the Indian Ocean and its international trade routes.

Kenya's roads carry about half of the country's freight traffic. On many roads, lorries, trucks, trailers and vans far outnumber cars. Vehicles drive on the left side of the road, as they do in Britain. Most towns and cities are connected by modern highways. However, many of the roads are in a very poor state of repair, with holes and cracked surfaces. Smaller towns and villages are linked by dirt roads. In the wet seasons, many of these roads become mud-baths that only four-wheel-drive vehicles can use.

Passengers wait on the platforms at the main railway station in Nairobi. ▼

Comparison of the length of the road and rail networks. ►►

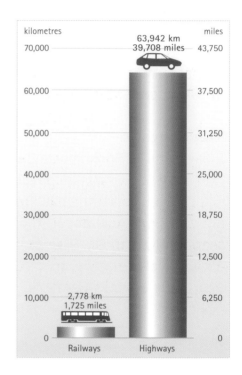

DATABASE

Buses and taxis

Cities and major towns have ample bus and taxi services. Buses range from modern, air-conditioned long-distance coaches to small local buses called *matatus*. Tourists travel mostly by coach or taxi or, on safari, by 4x4 or minibus. Kenyans are more likely to travel by matatu or pick-up trucks fitted with seats. In small towns, there are also bicycle taxis called *boda-bodas*.

Rail and sea

Kenya's railways consist of a main line from Mombasa to Nairobi and on into Uganda, with branch lines going off to Nyeri, Kitale and Kisumu. However, like the roads, the railway tracks have not been properly maintained. Delays, breakdowns and accidents have become commonplace. A series of accidents in the 1990s and 2000 led to almost all passenger services being suspended in 2001. The main lines are constantly used for freight.

Travel by air

Kenya's links with other countries outside Africa depend on its international airports and seaports. More than 30 airlines provide international air services between Kenya and Europe, Asia and the Middle East. Kenya's main seaport, Mombasa, also handles most of the import and export traffic for Uganda and northern Tanzania. Ships from here travel to Europe, Asia and other parts of Africa.

DATABASE

Airports

Kenya has two international airports – Jomo Kenyatta International Airport at Nairobi and Moi International Airport at Mombasa. Nairobi's second airport, Wilson Airport, handles flights within Kenya and to neighbouring countries. There are smaller airports at Diani, Eldoret, Kisumu, Kiwaiyu, Malindi and Lamu, and many airstrips used by light aircraft.

Mombasa

Mombasa is actually an island in a natural bay. Road and rail causeways link it to the mainland. A modern harbour takes up most of its western side. There is also a major oil refinery. An older harbour on its east coast is still used by Arab dhows and other small boats.

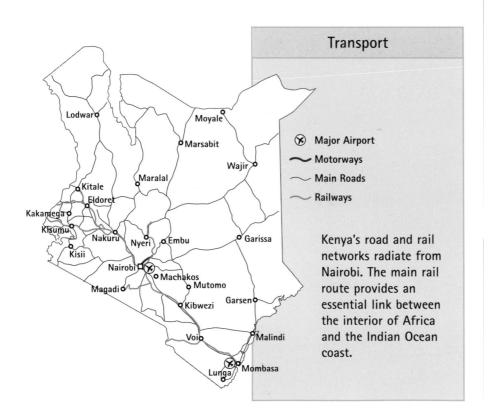

Transport

 Major Airport

Motorways

Main Roads

Railways

Kenya's road and rail networks radiate from Nairobi. The main rail route provides an essential link between the interior of Africa and the Indian Ocean coast.

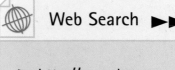 **Web Search** ►►

► http://www.kenya-airways.com
The website of Kenya Airways, Kenya's national airline.

Education

Language

For many children, especially in rural areas, their first language is the local tribal language that they speak at home. Their second language is Swahili. However, English is the language most widely used in commerce and education, so children are often taught it as their third language.

Kenya offers its citizens an education system that stretches from primary school all the way through to university. However, few Kenyans can afford to educate their children beyond primary school.

The school day in Kenya is longer than in many other countries. School begins at 8.00 or 8.30 in the morning and continues until about 4.00 in the afternoon. Teaching is usually formal, with children sitting at desks and classes focusing on literacy and numeracy. Primary education lasts for 8 years. It is provided free of charge by the government. Then students have to pass the KCPE (Kenya Certificate of Primary Education) examination before they can go on to 4 years at secondary school.

Town and country schools

Schools in the biggest cities and towns are usually well-funded, but rural schools often struggle for support. Community schools called harambee schools have sprung up in large numbers in rural areas. *Harambee* is Swahili and means 'pull together'. The government provides a teacher and the local community provides the building. Harambee schools now outnumber state-built schools.

◄◄ A class in a primary school. Kenyan schools are formal – pupils usually have to wear school uniform.

Adult education is increasing, helping those Kenyans who had to leave school early. Here, two new mothers are given an illustrated talk on family planning.

Higher education

For those who can go on to higher education, there are universities and colleges offering degree and diploma courses in academic subjects, professions and practical skills.

Kenya's leading higher education institutes include the University of Nairobi, Kenyatta University, Moi University, Kenya Polytechnic, the Jomo Kenyatta College of Agriculture and Technology, Kenya Medical Training College and Mombasa Polytechnic.

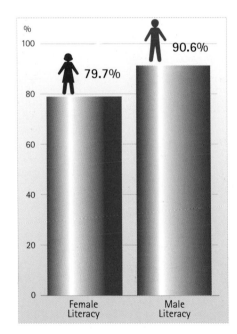

A comparison of the literacy rate of Kenyan males and females.

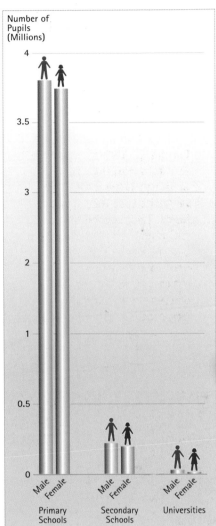

Few children get further than primary school.

Sport and Leisure

Kenya's sportsmen and women have achieved their greatest successes in athletics. For more than 10 years its middle-distance and long-distance runners have been among the best in the world.

Runners such as Kip Keino, Henry Rono, Moses Kiptanui and Wilson Kipketer have all won Olympic medals. In 2005, Martin Lel won the London Marathon, Philip Manyim won the Berlin Marathon and Catherine Ndereba won the Women's Boston Marathon for the fourth time.

In Kenya itself, a variety of sports are played. Football, cricket, rugby union, basketball, netball, volleyball and badminton are all popular. The country also hosts one of the World Car Rally Championship events – the gruelling Safari Rally of Kenya.

Marine Reserves

Kenya's coast is a major tourist attraction. The wildlife on the offshore reefs is every bit as spectacular as the animals on dry land. The reefs are protected by a series of marine parks and reserves where fishing is illegal and where tourists can dive to enjoy the underwater scenery. They are located at Lamu, Watamu, Malindi, Mombasa and Shimoni.

Kenyan long-distance runners often train in rural areas, running beside roads or along tracks in the grasslands. ▼

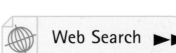
Tourists 'on safari' in Samburu
Game Reserve, looking for wildlife to
photograph.

Music

Kenya developed its own distinctive pop music, called
benga, during the 1960s and 1970s. Benga is still popular,
but today it competes with the European and American
pop, rock and rap music played by radio stations.
Traditional tribal music still exists in rural areas, but it has
largely been replaced by Christian gospel music.

Tourism

Kenya receives about a million visitors every year. They
make tourism Kenya's second-biggest export earner after
agriculture. Many of the tourists are attracted by game
parks and wildlife reserves. The most popular parks
include Amboseli, Tsavo East and Tsavo West, but there
are many others. The Nairobi National Park, on the
capital's doorstep, is a favourite with tourists who can visit
it in a day-trip from their hotels. Game reserves include
the famous Masai Mara and Samburu reserves.

Web Search ▶▶

▶ http://www.kws.org
Kenya Wildlife Service.

▶ http://www.awf.org
*Website of the African Wildlife
Foundation with lots of information
about Kenya's wildlife.*

▶ http://www.sporting-
heroes.net/athletics-
heroes
*Select the Kenyan flag to find out
more about Kenya's sporting heroes.*

Daily Life and Religion

Kenya's constitution allows for religious freedom. About two-thirds of the population are Christian. A small proportion are Muslim. Traditional African beliefs are still practised widely.

Traditional beliefs vary a great deal from one ethnic group, or tribe, to another. They often involve a belief in the existence in everyday life of spirits and ghosts. Believers do their best to keep the spirits happy in order to ensure success in their life and work. Witchcraft and magic are widely believed and practised, too.

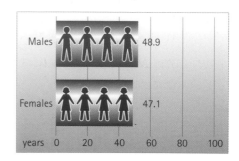

▲ Life expectancy has improved, but is still poor compared to more developed countries.

:::::::: DATABASE ::::::::

Food

Traditional Kenyan food is a mixture of African and Indian dishes. The African dishes include *ugali* (a type of cornmeal porridge). Indian dishes include *samosas* (fried triangular pastries) and *chapatis* (thin, flat bread). In the towns and cities, fast food shops selling burgers and fries are increasingly popular with teenagers who have money to spend.

◄◄ A young woman carries her baby on her back in a colourful sling as she shops in a local street market.

Shopping

In towns and cities, most shops open from 9.00 a.m to 6.00 p.m. Indoor and outdoor markets sell a wide variety of foods and goods. The stalls sell basic everyday needs and also carvings, jewellery and paintings aimed at tourists. Goods rarely have a fixed price. Shopping, especially in markets, involves the ritual of bargaining. The seller suggests a price that is far higher than the true value of the goods. The buyer offers to pay a ridiculously low sum. More prices are suggested and rejected until an agreed price is reached.

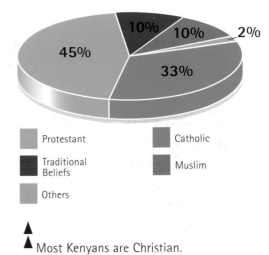

- 45% Protestant
- 10% Traditional Beliefs
- 10% Catholic
- 2% Muslim
- 33% Others

Most Kenyans are Christian.

The highly ornate outside of the Jamie Mosque – a Muslim place of prayer – in Nairobi. ▶▶

DATABASE

Missionaries

Religion in Kenya changed dramatically at the end of the 19th century. European missionaries used the newly built railway to travel inland. They converted many of the tribes they found from their traditional beliefs to Christianity. The results of their work can still be seen today in the religious mix of modern Kenya.

Web Search ▶▶

▶ http://www.state.gov/ g/drl/rls/irf/2001/ 5576.htm
Information about religion in Kenya from the US Department of State.

Arts and Media

Music, writing, dance and art are important in Kenyan culture. They keep alive historic customs and cultures, and pass them on to new generations. Traditional dance, music and drumming are still performed in rural areas.

Modern writing often deals with the lives of ordinary people and the country's politics. One of the most famous Kenyan writers is Ngugi wa Thiong'o. Local broadcasting is increasingly supplemented with satellite services, especially in hotels, bars and the homes of better-off urban families.

Newspapers

Kenya has lively and wide-ranging newspapers and magazines. *The Daily Nation* is the leading daily newspaper. It is also available online, as is the weekly *East African*. Most newspapers and magazines are published in English and there is a growing number of Swahili publications.

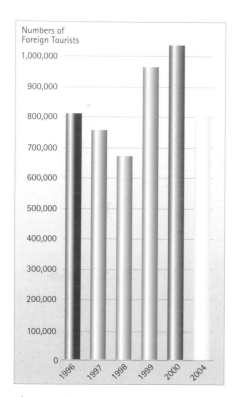

Number of foreign tourists visiting Kenya. Most tourists come to see the wildlife, relax on the beaches or visit the museums in Nairobi, but others come to experience the music, customs and traditions of Kenya.

A collection of hand-carved and painted figures, masks and souvenirs in traditional Kenyan style. ▶▶

▲ The modern concrete-and-glass *Daily Nation* newspaper building in Nairobi.

The total number of radio and television broadcasting stations. ▶▶

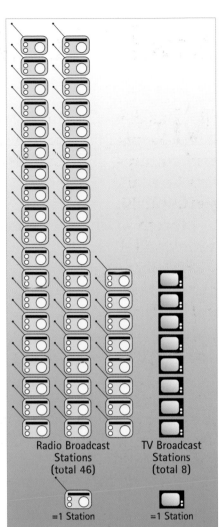

Radio Broadcast Stations (total 46)

TV Broadcast Stations (total 8)

 =1 Station

 =1 Station

Museums and galleries

Kenya's museums and historical sites receive more than half a million visitors each year. The National Museum in Nairobi has collections showing the vast variety of Kenya's plant and animal life, and its history, art and people. The Gedi ruins, near the coast between Malindi and Watamu, are the remains of a town deserted in the 17th century. Visitors can walk among the buildings. Fort Jesus in Mombasa, built by the Portuguese in the 16th century, is also popular with visitors. Prehistoric sites are numerous in Kenya. Some of them, including Olorgesailie near Nairobi and Kariandusi near Nakuru, are open to the public.

Architecture

Kenyan architecture ranges from traditional timber-framed homes to modern concrete and glass buildings. Traditional homes are made from a wooden frame covered with mud or dung. The modern buildings of central Nairobi are completely different. The most recognizable building in Nairobi is the tall cylindrical KANU tower at the Kenyatta Conference Centre. Near the coast, Arab and Portuguese influence is clear in some of the older buildings.

Web Search ▶▶

▶ http://www.museums.or.ke
The website of the National Museums of Kenya, with details of the Nairobi and regional museums and the country's historic sites.

▶ http://www.kenyadaily.com
Website of the Kenya Daily newspaper.

▶ http://www.eastandard.net
Website of the East African Standard.

▶ http://www.kbc.co.ke
Website of the Kenya Broadcasting Corporation.

Government

From 1895 until independence in 1963, Kenya was governed by Great Britain. The modern Republic of Kenya is led by a president who is both the head of state and the head of the government. The Cabinet – the group of politicians who govern the country – is appointed by the President.

The Kenyan Parliament has one chamber, called the National Assembly, or *Bunge*. It has 222 seats. Of these, 210 are elected by the people for a 5-year term. The president appoints the remaining 12 members according to the numbers of votes cast for the various parties. The president also appoints the vice-president.

Birth and death rates compared to the UK and USA.

Kenya has a high birth rate but, because of a struggling health service, a high rate of death among the newborn. ▼

	Births per 1,000 People	Deaths per 1,000 People	Infant Mortality (Deaths per 1,000 Live Births)
Kenya	40	15	61
UK	11	10	5
USA	14	8	7

◄◄ A statue of Jomo Kenyatta, Kenya's first president, in front of the Law Courts in Nairobi.

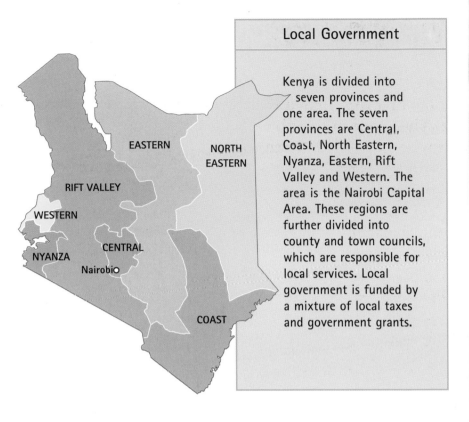

Local Government

Kenya is divided into seven provinces and one area. The seven provinces are Central, Coast, North Eastern, Nyanza, Eastern, Rift Valley and Western. The area is the Nairobi Capital Area. These regions are further divided into county and town councils, which are responsible for local services. Local government is funded by a mixture of local taxes and government grants.

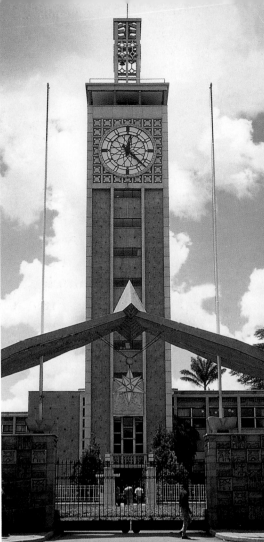

The Parliament Building in Nairobi. ▶▶

Presidential control

The president is elected from the members of the National Assembly by the people and serves for five years. To become president, a candidate must receive the largest number of votes and also win at least 25 per cent of the votes in five of Kenya's eight administrative divisions.

While Kenya's first President, Jomo Kenyatta, was in power, the country became a one-party state ruled by the Kenya African National Union (KANU). When Daniel Arap Moi became president after Kenyatta's death, one-party rule continued. The high level of corruption in the country prompted foreign governments and organizations to suspend aid in 1991. One-party rule was scrapped at the end of the year. However, corruption is still a major problem, as are terrorist threats.

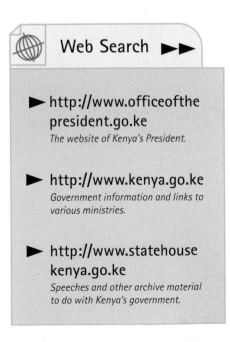

Web Search ▶▶

▶ http://www.officeofthe
president.go.ke
The website of Kenya's President.

▶ http://www.kenya.go.ke
Government information and links to various ministries.

▶ http://www.statehouse
kenya.go.ke
Speeches and other archive material to do with Kenya's government.

Place in the World

Chronology of Historical Events up to CE 1900

2000 BCE
People migrate south from Ethiopia and settle in Kenya

500 BCE–CE 500
People from Sudan migrate into Kenya

600
Arabs settle along the coast of East Africa

11th century
Mombasa is founded by Arab traders

1498
Portuguese explorers led by Vasco da Gama are the first Europeans to visit East Africa, arriving at Mombasa

1505
Mombasa is destroyed by the Portuguese

1528
A Portuguese fleet returns to attack the newly re-built Mombasa

1591
Warriors from Mombasa set out to attack Malindi. They are defeated. The victors hand Mombasa back to the Portuguese

1593–5 Fort Jesus is designed by an Italian architect and built at Mombasa by the Portuguese

1698
The Portuguese lose Mombasa to a 3,000-strong force from Oman

1729
Arabs drive the Portuguese out of East Africa

1895
The British East Africa Protectorate is formed, with Mombasa as its capital

Although people have long lived in East Africa, the modern independent Republic of Kenya is a young country just a few decades old. The new country's population has grown so fast that it has outstripped the government's ability to meet all of its needs. Now, though, the rate of population growth is decreasing.

Kenya has good relations with its neighbours. Its only border dispute concerns a wedge of land on its northern border, called the Elemi Triangle. This land, more than 10,000 square kilometres in area, is administered by Kenya, but also claimed by Sudan and Ethiopia.

▲ The traditional way of life of people such as the Masai are under threat as Kenya struggles to stay a major player in African politics and economics.

International links

Kenya is a member of many international organizations, including the United Nations (UN), the United Nations Educational, Scientific and Cultural Organization (UNESCO), the World Health Organization (WHO) and Interpol. It belongs to a number of co-operative organizations in Africa, including the African, Caribbean and Pacific group of states (ACP) and the African Union (AU).

As a country that was once governed by Great Britain, Kenya is also a member of the Commonwealth.

▲▲ Trucks from the UN High Commission for Refugees take displaced Ethiopians home from eastern Kenya.

A comparison of Kenya's imports and exports. ▼▼

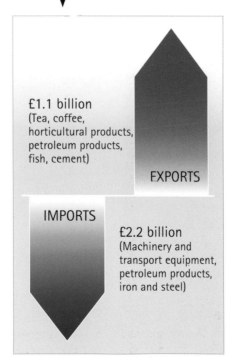

£1.1 billion
(Tea, coffee, horticultural products, petroleum products, fish, cement)

EXPORTS

IMPORTS

£2.2 billion
(Machinery and transport equipment, petroleum products, iron and steel)

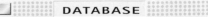

Chronology of Historical Events from 1900

1905
Nairobi becomes the capital of the British East Africa Protectorate

1920
The coast becomes the Protectorate of Kenya and the interior becomes the Kenya Colony

1952
The Mau Mau, a guerrilla group, begin a terror campaign against white settlers

1953
Jomo Kenyatta is jailed for his involvement with the Mau Mau

1959
Jomo Kenyatta is released

1963
Kenya becomes independent

1964
Kenya becomes a republic with Jomo Kenyatta as president

1978
Jomo Kenyatta dies. Daniel Arap Moi succeeds him as president

1982
The Air Force tries to seize power but fails

1991
Multi-party politics is restored

1992
Daniel Arap Moi is re-elected president

1998
A terrorist bomb explodes at the US Embassy in Nairobi, killing 250

2002
Britain pays tribespeople $7 million for deaths and injuries caused by explosives left on their land

2005
Government proposes a new constitution

Area:
582,650 sq km

Population size:
34,000,000 (2005 estimate)

Capital city:
Nairobi (population 2,343,000)

Other major cities:
Mombasa (660,000)
Nakuru (300,000)
Kisumu (160,000)
Eldoret (144,900)
Malindi (140,000)

Longest river:
Tana (708 km)

Largest lakes:
Lake Victoria (69,484 sq km)
Lake Turkana/Rudolf (6,405 sq km)

Highest mountain:
Mount Kenya (5,199 m)

Currency:
Kenya shilling (Ksh)
1 Kenya shilling = 100 cents

Flag:
Three horizontal bands of black, red and green, with thin white lines between them and a warrior's

shield over crossed spears at the centre

Languages:
Swahili (official), English, Kikuyu, Luo, Kamba

Major resources:
Limestone, soda ash, salt, fluorspar

Major exports:
Tea, coffee, horticultural products, petroleum products, fish, cement

National holidays and major events:
January 1: New Year's Day
May 1: Labour Day

June 1: Madaraka Day (celebrating self-government in 1960)
October 10: Moi Day
October 20: Kenyatta Day
December 12: Jamhuri (Independence Day)
December 25: Christmas Day
December 26: Boxing Day
Islamic festivals and holy days are observed too, but they are determined by the Islamic lunar calendar, so they fall on different dates each year.

Religions:
Christian, Muslim, traditional African beliefs

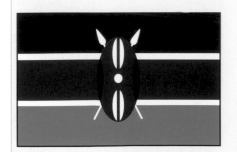

Glossary

AGRICULTURE
Farming the land, including ploughing, planting, raising crops, and raising animals.

ALTITUDE
The height of a mountain or an area of land above sea level.

BIRTH RATE
The number of babies born in a year compared to a set number of people, usually the number of babies born per 1,000 people in the population.

CASH CROP
A crop grown for sale, especially to another country.

CLIMATE
The average weather conditions experienced in an area over a long period of time.

CULTURE
The beliefs, ideas, knowledge and customs of a group of people, or the group of people themselves.

ECONOMY
A country's finances.

EQUATOR
The imaginary line round the centre of the Earth, dividing it into the northern and southern hemisphere, or halves.

EXPORTS
Products, resources or goods sold to other countries.

GEOTHERMAL POWER
Electricity generated by using natural underground heat to make steam for driving generators.

GOVERNMENT
A group of people who manage a country, deciding on laws, raising taxes and organizing health, education and other national systems and services.

GROSS DOMESTIC PRODUCT
The value of all goods and services produced by a nation in a year.

IMPORTS
Products, resources or goods brought into the country.

LITERACY
The ability to read and write.

LITERACY RATE
The percentage of the population who can read and write.

MANUFACTURING
Making large numbers of the same things by hand or, more commonly, by machine.

POPULATION
All the people who live in a city, country, region or other area.

POPULATION DENSITY
The average number of people living in each square kilometre of a city, country, region or other area.

RESOURCES
Materials that can be used to make goods or electricity, or to generate income for a country or region.

RURAL
Having the qualities of the countryside, with a low population density.

SUBURBS
Areas of housing between a city centre and the countryside.

URBAN
Having the qualities of a city, with a high population density.

Index